Teach It!
Instructional Activities

for

Temple, Ogle, Crawford, and Freppon

All Children Read
Teaching for Literacy in Today's Diverse Classrooms

Second Edition

with Research Navigator™ Access Code

Jean Wallace Gillet
Orange County (VA) Public Schools

with

Codruta Temple
Syracuse University

Boston   New York   San Francisco
Mexico City   Montreal   Toronto   London   Madrid   Munich   Paris
Hong Kong   Singapore   Tokyo   Cape Town   Sydney

To obtain permission(s) to use the material from this work, please submit a
written request to Allyn and Bacon, Permissions Department, 75 Arlington
Street, Boston, MA 02116 or fax your request to 617-848-7320.

ISBN 10: 0-205-54354-5
ISBN 13: 978-0-205-54354-0

Printed in the United States of America

10 9 8 7 6 5 4 3 2   11 10 09 08

Table of Contents

Reading Activities for Emergent and Beginning Readers

1.	Reading Aloud	1
2.	Dialogic Reading	3
3.	Language Experience or Group Dictated Story	4
4.	Language Experience with Authentic Children's Literature	5
5.	Big Book Lesson	7
6.	Making Individual Small Books	9
7.	Modified Reading Recovery Lesson	10
8.	Guided Reading	11
9.	Guided Reading and the Four Blocks Approach	12
10.	Shared Reading	13

Word Study Activities

11.	Phonemic Segmentation with Elkonin Boxes	14
12.	Beginning Sounds Picture Sorting	15
13.	Word Sorting	16
14.	Word Hunts	17
15.	Making and Breaking Words	18
16.	Word Wall Activities	19
17.	Analytic Phonics Lesson	20

Vocabulary Activities

18.	"Word Conversations" for Primary Grades	21
19.	Semantic or Concept Web for Upper Grades	22
20.	Connect Two	23
21.	Semantic Feature Analysis	24

Fluency Activities

22.	Repeated Reading	25
23.	Readers' Theater	26
24.	Choral Reading	27

Comprehension Activities with Fictional Texts

25. Terms in Advance   28
26. Directed Reading-Thinking Activity (DRTA)   29
27. Dual-Entry Diary   30
28. Save the Last Word for Me   31
29. Literature Circles   32
30. Discussion Web   33
31. Story Maps   34
32. Character Clusters and Character Maps   35

Comprehension Activities with Nonfictional Texts

33. Think-Pair-Share   36
34. Anticipation Guide   37
35. Graphic Organizers   38
36. Know – Want to Know – Learn (K-W-L)   39
37. What? So What? Now What?   40
38. Reciprocal Teaching   41

Writing Activities

39. Shared Writing   42
40. Interactive Writing   43
41. Pillowcase or Me in a Box   44
42. The Writing Workshop   45
43. Descriptive Writing   47
44. Story Maps for Writing   48
45. Form Poems   49

Activities for English-Language Learners

46. Language Experience with English-Language Learners   50
47. Cumulative Semantic Map   52
48. Word Origins and Derivations   53
49. Visualization   54
50. Using Questions to Teach English-Language Learners   55

Overview

This edition of *Teach It!* is designed to accompany the text *All Children Read: Teaching for Literacy in Today's Diverse Classrooms.* The lesson plans follow the order of their presentation in the text. They are designed for implementation by preservice teachers or by teacher education students in a practicum setting. They include a wide variety of activities featuring oral language development, emergent and beginning reading skills and concepts, reading comprehension, writing, and vocabulary development. Each of the activities is discussed in detail in the text.

Most of the featured lessons are intended for small group instruction within a regular classroom, and most can be readily adapted for individuals or larger groups, including whole classes. They provide opportunities for preservice teachers to practice instructional planning, lesson implementation, and classroom management while helping students develop critical language and literacy skills.

Each lesson plan includes a statement of objectives, stating what the activity is intended to teach or develop; a list of necessary materials, which should be gathered beforehand; and an estimated duration, or length of the lesson. Most lesson plans also include a list of suggested variations or extensions, which can be used to provide variety in subsequent lessons and to extend and enrich the learning experience. These can themselves become subsequent lessons, guided practice activities, or independent learning activities.

Each of these lessons can easily be modified to meet the individual needs of the preservice teacher, the supervising teacher, and the students in the classroom. Group size can be adapted and procedures and instructions can be modified to fit the needs and abilities of the students. Each activity is specific to one or more fundamental literacy skills, but each is also generic in that it can be productively retaught by changing the literature selection, writing stimulus, discussion props, and so forth. Each activity is one that preservice teachers should be familiar with and able to implement in the classroom.

Guidelines for Lesson Planning

- Plan every lesson ahead of time. Your mental preparation will enable you to present your lesson with skill and confidence. Planning ahead ensures that all necessary materials are at hand, allowing you to focus more on the students than on yourself.

- Select lessons to implement based on students' learning needs, not on your interests, strengths, or time constraints. Every lesson has an instructional purpose; knowing it will increase your confidence and enthusiasm.

- Collect and check all materials, supplies, and equipment beforehand. Missing markers, a mislaid book, or a burned-out overhead projector bulb can sabotage the best lesson.

- Be a positive language and literacy role model. Use precise, correct language, model enthusiasm for reading and literature, and show your enjoyment of learning.

- Reinforce positive behavior and effort by specifically drawing attention to what students did, rather than using empty praise. Point out when students use a strategy, attempt something difficult, or persist when having difficulty.

- Whenever possible, allow students choices, even if the range of choices is narrow. Having choices increases students' feeling of ownership and empowerment. Encourage diversity in answers to questions, ways to show comprehension, and choices of literature.

- Encourage and foster personalization and creativity. Show that you value students' attempts to relate what they are learning about to their own lives and experiences.

- Be prepared to handle interruptions, schedule changes, and the unforeseen with poise. No lesson ever unfolds exactly as planned, and an unexpected outcome can be even better than the planned outcome! Each lesson is a journey, and the "getting there" is as important as the destination.

- Evaluate each lesson you teach, even if your evaluation is only a brief self-reflection. If possible, jot down a few notes about what went well and what you'd do differently another time in a personal journal. Self-evaluation is one key to improving your teaching.

Using Research Navigator™

This edition of the *Teach It!* booklet for *All Children Read* is designed to integrate the content of the book with the valuable research tool, Research Navigator™, a collection of research databases, instruction, and contemporary publications available to you online at www.researchnavigator.com.

In the "Connect with Research" section at the end of every chapter in *All Children Read,* you'll see special prompts cuing you to visit the Research Navigator™ Web site to use the key terms in each chapter to expand on the concepts of the text and to further explore the work being done in the field of Reading and Literacy. To gain access to Research Navigator™, go to www.researchnavigator.com and log in using the personal access code you'll find on the inside front cover of the *Teach It!* booklet. RN learning aids include the following:

EBSCO's ContentSelect Academic Journal Database

EBSCO's ContentSelect Academic Journal Database contains scholarly peer-reviewed journals. These published articles provide you with a specialized knowledge and information about your research topic. Academic journal articles adhere to strict scientific guidelines for methodology and theoretical grounding. The information obtained in these individual articles is more scientific than information you would find in a popular magazine, newspaper article, or on a Web page.

The New York Times Search by Subject Archive

Newspapers are considered periodicals because they are issued in regular installments (e.g., daily, weekly, or monthly) and provide contemporary information. Information in periodicals—journals, magazines, and newspapers—may be useful, or even critical, for finding up-to-date material or information to support specific aspects of your topic. Research Navigator™ gives you access to a one-year "search by subject" archive of articles from one of the world's leading newspapers—*The New York Times.*

"Best of the Web" Link Library

Link Library, the third database included on Research Navigator™, is a collection of Web links, organized by academic subject and key terms. Searching on your key terms will provide you a list of five to seven editorially reviewed Web sites that offer educationally relevant and reliable content. The Web links in Link Library are monitored and updated each week, reducing your incidence of finding dead links.

In addition, Research Navigator™ includes extensive online content detailing the steps in the research process including:

- Starting the Research Process

- Finding and Evaluating Sources

- Citing Sources

- Internet Research

- Using Your Library

- Starting to Write

For more information on how to use Research Navigator™, go to
http://www.ablongman.com/aboutrn.com

Reading Activities for Emergent and Beginning Readers

1. Reading Aloud

Objectives: To develop children's ability to comprehend written language; to raise children's awareness of the structure of different types of texts; to expand children's vocabulary; to encourage enthusiasm for literacy

Materials: An age-appropriate book

Duration: 10–15 minutes

1. Prepare to read the book.
   a. Read the book through yourself before you read it to the children to decide whether it is suitable for your class.
   b. Decide how you want to read it—with humor, with drama, with questions to whet curiosity.
   c. If there are voices to bring to life, decide how you want to make each one sound.
   d. If you decide to stop reading to ask for predictions or for discussion, decide where the stopping places should be.
   e. If there are any words or ideas that will be unfamiliar to the children, make a note to pronounce them carefully and explain them to the children.
   f. If the book has illustrations large enough for the children to see, practice reading the book through while you hold it in front of and facing away from you, where the children will be able to read it.
2. Prepare the children.
   a. Make sure the children are seated comfortably where they can see and hear you.
   b. Remind the children, if you need to, of the behavior you expect of good listeners: hands to themselves, eyes on the teacher, and ears for the story.
3. Read the title.
4. Show the children the cover of the book, ask them what they know about the topic, and ask them to make predictions about what will happen or what they expect to find out in the book.

5. Turn to the title page. Read the author's name and the illustrator's. Talk about what each contributed to the book. Remind the children of any other books they know by this author or this illustrator.

6. As you read the book through the first time, ask for comments about what is going on and for predictions about what will happen.

7. Follow up the reading with a whole-class discussion about the book.

8. Read the book a second time through, taking more time to look at the illustrations and to talk about characters, their motives, or other things you and the students find interesting about the book.

9. Leave the book available to the children in the library corner, and encourage them to read it later during scheduled time in the reading center or between other activities. The children might especially enjoy taking turns reading it to each other.

2. Dialogic Reading

Objectives: To develop children's oral language and concepts about print

Materials: An age-appropriate book

Duration: 10–15 minutes

A. Dialogic reading for younger children (PEER)

1. Prompt the child to name objects in the book and talk about the story.

2. Evaluate the child's responses and offer praise for adequate responses and alternatives for inadequate ones.

3. Expand on the child's statements with additional words.

4. Ask the child to repeat the adult's utterances.

B. Dialogic reading for older children (CROWD)

While reading the book to the child, ask the following types of questions:

1. Completion questions. Ask the child to supply a word or phrase that has been omitted. (For example, "I see a yellow duck looking at ___.")

2. Recall questions. Ask the child about things that occurred earlier in the book. ("Do you remember some animals that Brown Bear saw?")

3. Open-ended questions. Ask the child to respond to the story in his or her own words. ("Now it's your turn: You say what is happening on this page.")

4. Wh- questions. Ask what, where, who, and why questions. ("What is that yellow creature called? Who do you think Brown Bear will see next?")

5. Distancing questions. Ask the child to relate the content of the book to life experiences. ("Do you remember when we saw a yellow duck like that one swimming in the lake? Was it as big as this one?")

3. Language Experience or Group Dictated Story

Objectives: To help emergent readers develop oral language fluency, print directionality, concept of word, sight word recognition, and phonemic awareness

Materials: An object, shared experience, favorite song or book, or other stimulus for the dictation; large chart tablet or 24 × 36-inch paper on easel or chalkboard; large marker

Duration: 10–30 minutes; additional time for follow-up activities listed below

1. Select a group of 4–10 children to participate.

2. Select and prepare stimulus for dictation: for example, an interesting concrete object, classroom pet, familiar story for retelling, recent classroom event.

3. Invite participants to gather close to the chart paper. Introduce activity by explaining that they will talk together about the stimulus and create statements about it that you will write for them on the chart paper. They will learn to read the sentences for themselves by rereading them together and pointing to the words.

4. Invite discussion of the stimulus, encouraging students to describe, narrate, and add verbal details. If necessary, ask open-ended questions like "What else do you notice?" "What else do you remember?" or "What happened after that?"

5. Ask for volunteers to contribute sentences for the dictation.

6. Write students' sentences verbatim, allowing changes or additions. Print neatly and clearly in large letters, with clear spaces between each word. Limit the account to 5–7 sentences.

7. Read the completed story expressively and at a natural pace, pointing to each word as you read.

8. Reread the story chorally several times until students have memorized it. Continue pointing to each word. (Keep up the pace so the reading sounds natural, not word by word.) If students have trouble memorizing the whole text, divide it into sections of two or three sentences each.

9. Invite volunteers to come to the chart and recite a part or the whole story while pointing to each word. Continue until each student who volunteers has read the story individually.

10. Point to individual words and invite students to identify the words, reading from the beginning to the target word if necessary.

4. Language Experience with Authentic Children's Literature

Objectives: To help emergent readers develop oral language fluency, print directionality, concept of word, sight word recognition, and phonemic awareness; to stimulate interest in and engagement with children's literature

Materials: A culturally appropriate piece of children's literature; chart paper or chalkboard; large marker or chalk

Duration: 15–30 minutes

1. As a stimulus for a language-experience dictation, conduct a read-aloud of a piece of children's literature that is culturally appropriate for your class.

2. During the read-aloud, share the illustrations in the book and ask questions about the unfolding story.

3. Have the children dictate their brief version of the story.

4. Accept the dictations of the children as stated, regardless of any cultural affectations, as long as other children do not suggest changes. However, spell the words correctly irrespective of students' pronunciation.

5. Make sure the children have many opportunities to read the text in a shared reading mode as the dictation is recorded and after the children's rendition of the story is completed.

6. Optionally, follow up with some of the activities suggested for the Language Experience or Group Dictated Story.

Follow-Up Activities for Group Dictated Story

- Repeat choral and individual reading and pointing on subsequent days until all students can read the story fluently and point accurately.

- Create an exact copy of the story on another sheet of chart paper. Cut the sentences or lines apart. Place in a center for students to reorder the lines and compare to the original.

- Copy each sentence onto a sentence strip. Have volunteers hold up each strip in correct order. (These can also be used for independent practice with a hanging pocket chart.)

- Create exact copies of the story on copy paper. Duplicate several copies for each participant. In different lessons, students can paste copies on construction paper or in journals and illustrate them, cut lines and sentences apart and put them in correct order, cut sentences into phrases and put them in correct order, and use sentences for handwriting practice.

- Have students find individual words they recognize in isolation and begin building individual word banks with known words on cards. Students should sort and review word banks daily.

- Have students sort words in their word banks in a variety of ways: matching beginning sounds, number of syllables, alphabetical order, and so forth.

- Select one or several familiar words beginning with consonants. Using individual letter cards or magnetic letters, show students how to "make and break" the words by removing the initial letter or sound and substituting another, creating new words (change THAT to HAT, PAT, RAT, and CAT; MATCH to PATCH, BATCH, and SCRATCH; MAKE to TAKE, RAKE, FAKE, and LAKE.)

- Have students write known sight words using magnetic letters on cookie sheets, individual letters cut out of sandpaper, wallpaper scraps, or felt, glue and sand or glitter, pipe cleaners, heavy yarn, macaroni letters, mini-marshmallows, dried beans, and so forth. (The more ways they practice making the same words, the more automatic these words will become!)

- Begin personal dictionaries by folding eight to ten sheets of paper vertically and stapling in the fold to create individual books. Have students write a letter at the top of each page (group infrequent letters like q, u, x, y, and z with others) and begin collecting mastered sight words in their dictionaries.

5. Big Book Lesson

Objectives: To help emergent readers develop familiarity with book language patterns, print directionality, concept of word, sight word recognition, and phonemic awareness

Materials: A big book of your choice; for follow-up activities, a Word Hider (index card), sentence strips, pocket chart

Duration: 10–30 minutes; additional time for follow-up activities listed below

1. Display the big book, closed, on an easel or display stand (so your hands are free). Invite students to gather close enough to the book so everyone can clearly see the print.

2. Read the title, pointing to the words, and encourage students' observations about the cover art. Invite predictions of what the book might be about or what might happen based on the title and cover.

3. Open to the title page and read the author's and illustrator's names, pointing to the words. Be sure everyone knows what the author and the illustrator did. Make connections to other familiar books by the author or illustrator, if appropriate.

4. Read the first page fluently and expressively, pointing to the words. Comment, or invite student comments, on the illustrations. Review previous predictions and have students revise or confirm predictions based on what is now known.

5. Repeat this step with each page, or several pages at a time, depending on the length and complexity of the text and the illustrations. Continue pointing to the words as you read. Continue inviting new or revised predictions as the story unfolds.

6. As you near the story's conclusion, invite final predictions of how it will end. Read to the end of the story.

7. Invite students' comments about the story and illustrations. Encourage them to talk about characters or story parts they liked, appealing illustrations, and so forth. You may wish to go back to particular illustrations to reexamine them, looking for details, or just for enjoyment.

Five-Day Plan for Using a Big Book

Day 1: Follow the preceding plan for the first reading. Goals for this lesson include introduction to the story, forming and revising predictions based on illustrations and unfolding plot, perusal of illustrations, and general enjoyment of the book activity.

Day 2: Either reread the story in its entirety, pointing to the words, or echo-read the story with students. (You read a sentence or two, pointing to the words, then students repeat verbatim or "echo.") At relevant points, stop to discuss predictions made during previous reading, and help students verbalize how they arrived at those predictions. Reexamine illustrations, this time for features overlooked the first time, details of colors, borders, and so forth. If appropriate, compare this book to familiar others by the same author or illustrator.

Day 3: Reread the story, inviting students to "chime in" or read along with you (choral-read) as desired. Some may be more ready to do so than others. Predictable lines, repeating refrains, and rhyming elements will support choral reading. Continue pointing to the words as you read. Emphasize comprehension in this lesson; ask questions about the story events, characters, setting, and so forth, inviting students to use both the text and illustrations to find information and justify their answers.

Day 4: Reread chorally, encouraging all students to read with you as much as they can. Many will have memorized the story by now. (If many are still unable to choral-read it, break the story into sections to work on.) Emphasize "word work" in this lesson. Point to and have volunteers identify selected words. Use the Word Hider (index card) to cover selected words, have students read from the beginning of the sentence and identify the hidden word; uncover to confirm. See how many times students can find the same word on the same and subsequent pages, find other words with the same beginning sound, or match words to familiar words on the Word Wall.

Day 5: Reread chorally, letting your voice "fade" so students are reading more independently. Have volunteers come forward to read one or more sentences, pointing to the words as they read. Distribute sentences on sentence strips and have students put them in order in pocket chart. Have students act out the story and/or do related art, cooking, or other extension activities to enrich the literary experience.

6. Making Individual Small Books

Objectives: To provide students with small easily read books they can read independently at school and home

Materials: Two sheets of 8½ × 11 plain paper for each student, supply of old magazines with colorful illustrations, scissors, glue, markers, stapler

Duration: 15–30 minutes, depending on number of students participating

1. Prepare a blank book for each student by placing two sheets of paper together, 11-inch side at top, folding vertically down the middle. Staple vertically in the fold, creating a book about 5½ × 8½ with front and back covers and six inner pages.

2. Select a group of six to eight students. For larger groups, another adult is needed to assist students. Give each student a magazine, or magazine pages with colorful pictures, and scissors.

3. Select a group of eight or fewer students. If group is larger, have another adult available to assist students. Gather around a work table where supplies have been placed.

4. Show students a premade model book: A magazine picture has been cut out and glued to each of the six pages of a book, and an adult has labeled the picture underneath with a simple phrase or sentence: "The dog is jumping," "A box is round," "A red apple," and so forth.

5. Assist students in choosing a picture and gluing it to the first page. Have them continue to complete the remaining pages. Using a marker, write the student's dictated sentence or phrase neatly and clearly under each picture. Have students copy a title onto the cover, print their names, and if desired write or draw on the back cover.

6. Assist each student in reading the entire book and practicing it so each can read his or her book fluently to the group or class during sharing time.

Variations: Give each book a theme and a title: Things That Are Round, What Is Square? (shapes); Red Is Everywhere, Things That Are Blue (colors), Animals All Around, Outdoors, We Can Play (various play activities), What Starts with B? (initial letters/sounds), It's Spring! (seasons or holidays), Foods We Love.

7. Modified Reading Recovery Lesson

Objectives: To help emergent readers develop oral language fluency, print directionality, concept of word, sight word recognition, and phonemic awareness

Materials: Individual copy of a short, predictable, clearly illustrated "little book" at Guided Reading levels A–D or Reading Recovery levels 1–8 for each participant

Duration: 10–15 minutes, depending on length and difficulty of text

1. Select one to three emergent readers to participate. (If more than one, have students take turns during the following steps.)

2. Preview the book by reading the title, encouraging student/s to examine cover illustration and predict what might happen or what the book might be about.

3. Guide student/s in looking at the illustration on each page, naming objects and/or describing the picture, and if necessary modeling expanded oral language by repeating students' remarks in expanded form (S: "A dog." T: Yes, there's a dog. It's a brown dog.")

4. Read and point to an important word or phrase, or repeated phrases, on each page as you examine the illustrations. ("T: "Here's the word *dog*.") In this way you smooth the way for the reader/s to read each page independently.

5. Return to the first page and invite the student/s to read each page as independently as possible. Provide assistance on unfamiliar words, and encourage the student/s to use the picture, beginning sounds, and sentence context to attempt unknown words. Point out strategies you observe the student/s using: "You were smart to go back and read that sentence again when you got stuck," "I saw you get your mouth ready to say the beginning sound," or "You did what good readers do when you looked at the picture."

6. Choral-read the book with the student/s one or more times to gain familiarity with the sound of the sentences being read smoothly.

7. Invite student/s to read the whole book one more time with less teacher support. Encourage the student/s to reread the book several times independently at school and/or at home for fluency.

8. Guided Reading

Objectives: To develop effective strategies for processing novel text at increasingly challenging levels of difficulty; to develop students' ability to read silently

Materials: Multiple copies of leveled books

Duration: 5 minutes prior to reading; time necessary to complete reading and to respond to the story

1. Select a group of 4–6 children who are reading at about the same level.

2. Introduce a new text at students' instructional level. Encourage the students to converse about the text, to ask questions, and to build expectations.

3. Have the children read the entire text, or a unified part of it, to themselves silently (or softly in the case of younger readers). Allow them to ask for help when needed.

4. While the students are reading, observe their problem-solving strategies and provide assistance by suggesting other suitable strategies.

5. After the reading, involve the children in responding to the story through such activities as writing, discussion, paired reading, or sharing personal responses.

6. For subsequent guided reading sessions, regroup the children in accordance with outcomes that you have observed and assessed.

9. Guided Reading and the Four Blocks Approach

Objectives: To develop effective strategies for processing novel text at increasingly challenging levels of difficulty; to develop children's ability to read silently; to increase children's writing fluency; to teach word study skills in a meaningful context

Materials: Multiple copies of leveled books; optionally, a big book; chart paper for whole-class word study activities

Duration: 40-60 minutes

A. Working with small groups

1. Follow steps 1–4 of the Guided Reading strategy as described earlier.

2. Have the students respond to the story in writing. Suggest writing prompts that are appropriate to students' level of writing development.

3. Follow the writing block with 10–15 minutes of self-selected reading time. Help students select texts at their independent reading level.

4. Teach word study skills tailored to the needs of the children in the group.

B. Working with the whole class

1. Make the text accessible to all students with multiple readings involving read-aloud, shared reading, and paired reading.

2. Have the students respond to the story in writing.

3. Follow the writing block with 10–15 minutes of self-selected reading time. Help students select texts at their independent reading level.

4. In the last block, do word study with the whole class, with all students working on the same skills, or, if possible, teach appropriate skills in smaller groups.

10. Shared Reading

Objectives: To develop comprehension by modeling comprehension strategies; provide guided practice in using comprehension strategies

Materials: Fiction or nonfiction book students will read together

Duration: 10–30 minutes depending on length of book and size of group

1. Select a text for students to read. A big book can be used with younger readers.

2. Select two or more comprehension strategies to demonstrate; for example, organizing prior information before reading, predicting story outcomes, creating good questions, visualizing scenes, self-monitoring comprehension, making inferences about information not directly stated, using context to understand new words, identifying and clarifying difficult parts, or summarizing.

3. Preview the book with students; examine the title and cover illustration, predict what the topic of the book might be or what might happen in the story, and look at each page, examining illustrations and pointing out important words.

4. After previewing, read the text to or with students, depending on how well they can handle the text. Students can read predictable or repeated parts, echo-read or choral-read, or alternate reading with you.

5. While reading, "think aloud" to model effective reading: Pause to wonder or predict what might happen next, tell what a part reminds you of, wonder about word meanings, demonstrate how to use word parts or context to figure out new words, identify and reread difficult parts, and comment on illustrations. Emphasize the strategies you selected beforehand. For example, if you selected visualizing, think aloud about how you are imagining the setting, characters, and action; if you selected inferring, demonstrate making an inference from several related facts or ideas. Model what good readers do as they read.

6. Invite students' comments and predictions about the text. Ask and invite thoughtful questions.

7. Reread the text in its entirety to "put the pieces together" and experience the material as a whole. With greater familiarity, students may be able to read more of the text themselves.

8. Make the text available for students to reread independently.

Word Study Activities

11. Phonemic Segmentation with Elkonin Boxes

Objectives: To develop phonemic awareness and ability to segment phonemes in words

Materials: Elkonin boxes (series of connected squares) drawn on paper or sentence strips: two boxes for words with two phonemes, and so forth; "counters" such as poker chips or dried lima beans for student to move; letter cards or magnetic letters

Duration: 5–10 minutes

1. Select a word with 2–4 phonemes (for example, *to, cat, trip*) to segment. Use the Elkonin box with the appropriate number of spaces. Say the word, then say the word phoneme by phoneme; as you say each phoneme, push or place a counter into a box. Have the student watch as you do this. If necessary, repeat.

2. Have the student copy what you did: Say the word, and then say each sound while pushing the counters into the boxes. If an error occurs, stop the student by placing your hand over his or hers and modeling again, saying, "Watch again. Now you try." Repeat until the student can segment the phonemes and place the counters correctly.

3. Repeat the process with another word. You may choose another word with the same number of phonemes (*to, in, at*) or proceed to a word with one more phoneme (*in, pin, spin*).

4. When the student has mastered segmenting the phonemes and moving the counters, begin using letter cards or magnetic letters instead of counters, placing the letters in the boxes. (Keep letters representing digraph sounds together; for example, *that* has three phonemes, and the letters *th* are placed together in the first box.)

5. When the student has mastered moving the letters into boxes, you can remove the boxes altogether and continue practicing using just the letters.

12. Beginning Sounds Picture Sorting

Objectives: To develop phonemic awareness, ability to distinguish among several different beginning sounds, and ability to categorize pictures of objects with same beginning sound

Materials: Set of commercial beginning sounds sorting cards, or teacher-made cards with clear pictures of common objects, six to eight of each of two or more initial consonant sounds; pocket chart

Duration: 10–15 minutes

1. Preselect two or more beginning consonant sounds that are clearly different; begin with two contrasting sounds, and add more as students gain familiarity with procedure. Select pictures of objects with these beginning sounds.

2. Gather a group of 4–10 students in front of the pocket chart.

3. Hold up each card and have students name each object. Be sure all students can name each object accurately.

4. Place one card for each sound at the top of the pocket chart. Tell students they will name the object on each card and place each card below the picture that begins with the same sound.

5. Mix up the remaining cards. Hold up each one and have students name the object chorally. Give each successive card to a different student. Have the student come to the chart, say a "sorting sentence" naming the two objects such as "Basket starts like baby," and place it in the correct column.

6. As each card is added to a column, have students name all the objects in that column chorally to check that they all have the same beginning sound.

7. When all pictures have been correctly sorted, have students name all the objects in each column one more time to reinforce the beginning sound. You may leave the cards near the pocket chart for students to sort independently as time allows.

Variations: Place one example of each sound at the top of the pocket chart. Distribute the remaining cards to students. Have students holding a card beginning with one sound come to the chart, say the sorting sentence, and place their cards in a column. Repeat with the other sound(s). Or dispense with the pocket chart: Have students line up next to each other, all the students with cards beginning with the same sound in one line. Have them name all the objects with the same beginning sound chorally.

13. Word Sorting

Objectives: To learn to discern patterns of similarity among words with similar sound, spelling, grammatical, or meaning patterns

Materials: Word cards with printed words that share a particular feature; pocket chart

Duration: 5–15 minutes, depending on number of words to sort and size of group

1. From a word wall, sight word banks, spelling list, or other source of words recognized at sight, select 2–4 features to contrast (for example, different beginning consonants, beginning blends, short or long vowel patterns, or parts of speech) and 4–6 words that share the same feature for each category. When introducing a new feature, or with struggling readers, contrast only two features at one time.

2. Review all the word cards with students; hold each up and have them identify the word chorally. Discard any words not recognized quickly.

3. Select one word from each group to represent the feature; read it and place it at the top of the pocket chart. Words sharing that feature will be placed below it in vertical columns. Point out the critical feature: "Let's find all the words that begin with the same sound as ball," ". . . have the same vowel sound as run," ". . . mean more than one," or ". . . are adjectives, words that describe things."

4. Mix up the remaining cards and hold each one up, having students read it aloud. Have volunteers come forward to place the word in the correct column and say the "sorting sentence"; for example, "Men means more than one man" or "Pretty is an adjective."

5. When all words have been correctly sorted, have students read each column chorally beginning with the example word.

6. Leave the example words displayed, remove and mix up the cards, and leave them near the pocket chart for independent sorting.

Variations: Have students sort their word banks and create their own individual sorts on the floor or table in front of them, using the example words you give them. Have students create their own individual sorts using word bank or word wall words, and let others guess the common feature. Have students sort their spelling words and write the words in categories as a practice exercise.

14. Word Hunts

Objectives: To develop children's ability to make connections between the spelling and the pronunciation of words

Materials: Chart paper

Duration: 10–15 minutes

1. Select a short rhymed poem and write it in large print on a piece of chart paper.

2. Read the poem to the children.

3. Read it a second time with the children reading along.

4. Have the children reread the poem in partner groups.

5. Ask the children what they notice about the words at the end of each line. Elicit examples of rhyming words.

6. Tell the children you want to go on a word hunt for two words that don't rhyme. Thinking aloud, select two words that don't rhyme and, on another piece of chart paper, write them as the headings of two columns.

7. Tell the students to copy the columns and the headings into their notebooks.

8. Organize the class in pairs.

9. Tell the children that each pair has to find as many rhyming words as they can that match the top word in each column. The words can be new ones that they think of, words from the word walls, and words in the poem.

10. Have the pairs share the words they have found.

11. Talk about what makes words rhyme.

15. Making and Breaking Words

Objectives: To develop phonemic awareness and ability to segment onset (beginning sound) and rime (the rest of the word without the beginning sound)

Materials: Magnetic letters or letter cards for students (metal cookie sheets for magnetic letters, and "letter holders" [sheet of paper folded 2 inches up from bottom and stapled vertically to create three or four pockets for letter cards] are helpful but optional); a large set of letter cards for demonstration

Duration: 10–15 minutes

1. Preselect two to four common phonograms that can become several different words by changing the initial consonant; these are often called "word families." Examples are *-an, -am, -ot, -ock, -in, -ake, -ike,* and *-ill.* Preselect letters for these phonograms and the beginning sounds.

2. Select a group of students. Each student needs a set of letters or cards to make the phonograms and the necessary beginning letters. Gather around a table so students can manipulate letters.

3. Use large letter cards on the table or in a pocket chart to demonstrate. Put up the letters necessary to make a word such as *man.* Then remove the M and substitute another letter, such as P. Ask students to read the new word, *pan.*

4. Have students repeat the procedure themselves, using the magnetic letters or letter cards. Have them say the initial word, then say the new word as the initial letter is substituted. On the display set, again remove the initial letter and substitute another such as R, this time asking, "What word did I make this time? That's right, *ran.* Use your letters to make *ran.*"

5. Continue until all real words have been made. (Avoid creating nonsense words like *zan.*)

6. Using the demonstration letters, quickly "make and break" all the words in one word family and have students read each word. Then have students use their letters to quickly make the words as you call them out. Repeat with the other word families used.

16. Word Wall Activities

Objectives: To develop automatic (sight) recognition of words

Materials: Large bulletin board or wall space for display of word collections, with room to add 5–10 new words per week; blank word cards or sentence strips; heavy black and/or colored markers

Duration: 2–3 minutes to introduce each new word; 10+ minutes for a daily review of all words

1. To create a word wall of high-utility sight words, select 5–10 high-utility or frequently occurring words per week that students can recognize; begin with the simplest, like *I*, *a*, *the*, *is*, *am*, and so forth, and continue adding words weekly as students encounter them over and over in reading and writing. Divide the word wall space alphabetically; use letter cards to create spaces so words can be added with others beginning with the same letter.

2. To add a new word, print the word in large neat letters on a letter card. Hold up the card and "say-and-spell" the word aloud: "Good. G-O-O-D. Good."

3. Have students say-and-spell chorally, clapping as they say each letter. Repeat if students had difficulty.

4. Print the word on the board, or trace each letter with your finger, spelling aloud as you go. Say the word again.

5. Have students print the word or trace the letters with their fingers on desktops, the floor, or the back of their other hand, spelling the word aloud as they write/trace and repeating the whole word.

6. Have students "help you" find the letter category the new word goes in, and attach it to the word wall. Say-and-spell it again in unison. Quickly review all the words in that letter category.

7. Review at least some of the word wall words daily; point to the word and say-and-spell chorally. Have students practice "reading the wall" independently throughout the day.

Variations: Instead of, or in addition to, sight words, word walls can be made of word families (*-ike*, *-op*, etc.); beginning consonants, blends, and digraphs; vowel patterns; plurals; synonyms and antonyms; parts of speech (adjectives, prepositions, etc.); unusual words; subject-area words (math, science, health, history, etc.), holidays; sports; music; homophones; contractions; base words with their derivational forms; prefixes and suffixes; words with related Latin and Greek bases (*bio-*, *tele-*, *graph*, etc.); and words from a particular work of literature.

17. Analytic Phonics Lesson

Objectives: To help students learn to recognize new words by analogy to similar known words; to help develop phonemic awareness

Materials: Chalkboard, chart paper, or transparency, or letter cards and pocket chart, or magnetic letters and cookie sheet

Duration: 5–10 minutes

1. Select a word students know that can become several different words by changing the initial consonant, or have a student suggest a word they know to make new words from.

2. Write and say the word. Then say, "If I know _____, I know _____" while you remove or cover the initial consonant or cluster and replace it with another. (For example, "If I know ship, I know slip.") Repeat the process while the students say, "If I know ___, I know ___."

3. Repeat with the other initial letters to continue making new words. Invite volunteers to come forward to move the letters and make new words while saying the sentence as above.

4. Have students practice with a partner making and reading new words using letter cards or magnetic letters.

Variations: Have students write all the new words they can make from one known word. Add words to the Word Wall as needed. As students are able to recognize the new words at sight, have them add them to their individual word banks. Have students use the new words in oral and written sentences. Add new words to personal dictionaries.

Vocabulary Activities

18. "Word Conversation" for Primary Grades

Objectives: Introduce students to new vocabulary; help students learn the pronunciation, meaning, and use of new words

Materials: A fiction or nonfiction book to read aloud to students; chalkboard or chart paper

Duration: 5–10 minutes for each new word taught; sufficient time to read the book aloud

1. Select a book featuring rich use of language to read to the class or group. Select one to three unfamiliar words to teach. Read the book to the group or class.

2. After the reading, print the new word on the board. Point to it as you put the new word into the context of the book by using the word in a sentence about the book; for example, "In this story (*Best Friends* by Steven Kellogg), Kathy wishes Louise would get a contagious disease so Louise could come home. Say that word with me: *contagious*." Point to the word as children repeat it.

3. Give a one-sentence definition of the word in terms the students can understand: "*Contagious* means that an illness is catching; you can catch it from someone else."

4. Give an example or two that children will be able to understand: "Colds are contagious; you can get a cold from someone else if that person sneezes or coughs near you and you breathe in the germs. Chicken pox is very contagious; if one child in a family gets it, usually the other children get it soon afterward."

5. Ask children to provide their own examples of the word: "I got chicken pox from my best friend in kindergarten." "When I got pinkeye I had to stay home because I was contagious for one day."

6. Have students echo as you say the word and its meaning again: "Contagious means that an illness is catching."

Extensions: Add the new word to a poster, bulletin board, "new word" Word Wall, or other display of interesting vocabulary words. Have students make up and act out brief skits to demonstrate the word's meaning. Have students write the new word and illustrate it. Have them add their illustration to individual vocabulary books they create and add to systematically. Designate it the "Word of the Day," and see how many ways students can use the word in meaningful sentences. Add the new word as a bonus word to the weekly spelling list.

19. Semantic or Concept Web for Upper Grades

Objectives: To learn specific meanings of synonyms and to categorize synonymous words by connotative meanings or shades of meaning

Materials: List of synonyms or words related by meaning; chalkboard, overhead transparency, or chart paper

Duration: 10–20 minutes, depending on number of synonyms and size of group

1. From a Word Wall, thesaurus, student writing, reading material, or other source, select a group of words sharing a common meaning; for example, these words relate to the concept of "more than enough": *plenty, excess, ample, lavish, copious, plethora, surfeit, myriad, superfluous, profuse.*

2. Write each word, pronounce it, and brainstorm with students what each one means. Provide several good context sentences to help them determine specific meanings.

3. Help students generate several categories into which the words can be sorted; for example, these words may suggest *many, enough,* and *too much.* Create a web on the board, transparency, or chart paper with circles or boxes that are large enough to write all the words in that category inside it. (Students often make their circles too small.) Or have students fold a sheet of paper to create the required number of boxes: in half for two, thirds for three, or quarters for four. They label each folded section and list the words in it that fit that category.

4. Have students sort the words into their appropriate categories; for example, "many" may include *lavish, ample, myriad, profuse, copious,* and *plethora*; "enough" may include *plenty* and *surfeit*; and "too much" may include *excess* and *superfluous.*

5. Have students come up with their own context sentences that illustrate the meanings of each word.

20. Connect Two

Objectives: Help students learn new vocabulary by predicting meanings of and relationships among key terms from a selection prior to reading

Materials: List of key terms from a selection to be read by students

Duration: 5–15 minutes depending on number and familiarity of terms selected

1. Preview a selection students will read. Collect five or more key terms from the selection, including technical vocabulary and unusual or unfamiliar uses of known words. List them on the board, a transparency, or duplicated worksheets.

2. Explain that all of the terms are used in the selection, and thinking about them before reading will help students recognize and understand them when they encounter them in the text. Pronounce each word.

3. Pair students and have each pair select two terms and use them together in a meaningful sentence. Sentences should, if possible, reflect what students think the words mean or how they are related.

4. Have students write their sentence for each pair of words and, if desired, draw a sketch to accompany it. Then have each pair share the sentences and comments about them with the larger group.

Variation: Instead of creating sentences, have students categorize terms they think go together, give each category a title or heading, and explain why they grouped them together when they share.

21. Semantic Feature Analysis

Objectives: To enrich vocabulary; help students relate a new concept to familiar concepts

Materials: Nonfiction text; chalkboard, chart paper, or transparency; marker

Duration: 10–15 minutes

1. Select a concept from a nonfiction text about which students may have limited prior knowledge or experience. Think of several related concepts about which students may know a little more to compare to it.

2. Create a chart on the board, chart paper, or transparency with a vertical (y) and a horizontal (x) axis. On the x-axis, list the new concept and the related concepts; on the y-axis, list several features of the concepts they may share.

3. Prior to reading, engage students in using what they may already know and their predictions to complete the chart. Start with the concepts they may be more familiar with, and ask if each feature is true; if the concept has that feature, mark it with a plus (+), and if the concept does not have that feature, with a minus (–). End with the new concept; students may not know if it has a particular feature but are to predict based on what they already know.

4. Have students complete the reading of the selection. Have them watch for information about the concept that they predicted about.

5. After reading, reexamine the chart. Have them compare their predictions about the new concept to what they learned from the reading, and change the chart as needed. Review what is now known about the new concept.

Fluency Activities

22. Repeated Reading

Objectives: To develop children's reading fluency

Materials: A reading passage of 50–500 words, depending on the child's reading rate

Duration: 10 minutes

1. Find a text (informational or fictional but not poetry or lists) written at the student's instructional level.

2. Sit next to the student in a quiet place, and listen as the student practices reading the text repeatedly.

3. Keep a copy of the text yourself on which you can mark the student's reading errors. (Errors are words that are omitted, or for which other words are substituted, or which are mispronounced. If the student does not say a word, wait 2 seconds and say the word yourself, and count that as an error.)

4. Time the student's reading for exactly 60 seconds, then stop the student, count the total number of words read, and subtract the errors from the total.

5. Have the student practice reading the text several times—preferably until the child reaches the criterion score for his or her grade level. Remember to offer adequate praise each time.

23. Readers' Theater

Objectives: To develop students' reading fluency and comprehension

Materials: A fictional text that contains dialogue, preferably among several characters

Duration: 15–25 minutes

1. Make a photocopy of the text you plan to use for readers' theater.

2. Read through the text and mark the parts that should be read by different readers. Create a code for different readers, such as a capital letter to represent the name of each different character, and a capital N followed by a number for narrator number 1, 2, 3, and so on.

3. Put brackets [ ] around the parts that will be read by each reader, and write in a letter over each section to indicate who should read it.

4. Strike through any parts that do not need to be read. Often "He said," "she replied," and the like, can be eliminated without affecting the meaning.

5. As they prepare to read a fictional text with readers' theater, have the students discuss the setting of the text, who the characters are, and what they are like.

6. Have the students read portions of the text several times in order to read the lines fluently and with the expression called for.

7. Offer coaching, asking the students questions such as,

   • "What is your character feeling right now? How do you sound when you feel that way? Should your voice be loud or soft? Fast or slow?"

   • "What might your character think about what the other character is saying? How will your character sound then?"

   • "What is going on at this point in the story? How is your character reacting to it?"

   • "How is your character changing as the story proceeds?"

8. Offer comments and suggestions after each practice reading and invite the students to do the same.

24. Choral Reading

Objectives: To develop reading fluency in a meaningful context

Materials: Poems with a strong rhythmic pattern

Duration: 10–15 minutes

1. Prepare the children to choral-read a text by discussing the circumstances or the context in which it might be said. Ask the children to imagine the situation and to describe the sounds they associate with it. Offer suggestions as necessary.

2. Decide how the poem should be read, for example, by the whole chorus, by individuals, by pairs, or by two alternating sections; in loud or soft voices; rapidly or slowly; melodiously, angrily, giggling, or seriously.

3. Have each student or group of students practice reading their part until they can keep the rhythm perfectly.

4. Have the whole class practice reading the poem in the manner previously agreed on until they sound like a good chorus. Invite and give feedback after each performance.

Comprehension Activities
with Fictional Texts

25. Terms in Advance

Objectives: To develop comprehension by recalling and organizing prior information before reading; enable students to predict what a reading passage might be about; familiarize students with key vocabulary and concepts prior to reading

Materials: List of key terms or phrases from the text to be read, chart paper or transparency, marker

Duration: 5–15 minutes, depending on size of group, number of terms, familiarity of terms

1. From a reading passage students are going to read, collect a group of key words and/or phrases that bear importantly on the content of the passage. Try to include both familiar and unfamiliar terms; don't just collect all the hardest or least familiar vocabulary.

2. Display the words on a chart or transparency with space around each one for recording students' ideas of what each term means and/or how it might bear on the passage they will read.

3. If your main goal for the activity is to encourage predictions about what the text to be read will be about, have students hypothesize about ways in which the terms might be related in the story. Optionally, you may allow them to write down their predictions before sharing them with the class. Accept all hypotheses or predictions encouragingly.

4. If your main goal is to introduce new vocabulary, have students dictate or write sentences explaining the meaning of one or more of the terms, or make up sentences that combine two or more of the terms in one sentence.

5. As students read the text and the meaning of various terms becomes clear, modify the chart or transparency to show what each term means in the passage and to reflect new information gained during reading. Alternatively, ask students to compare the story they read to their initial predictions.

26. Directed Reading-Thinking Activity (DRTA)

Objectives: To develop comprehension by recalling and organizing prior information before reading

Materials: Fiction selection; chalkboard, chart paper, or transparency; marker

Duration: 10–30 minutes or longer, depending on length of selection

1. Select a story with a well-structured plot that revolves around a character's attempts to solve a problem or achieve a goal, with a clear resolution of the conflict at the end.

2. Plan from two to five stopping points in the story, where students will stop reading to discuss what they have read and make predictions about forthcoming parts of the story. Plan the stops just before some major event or piece of information.

3. Explain to students that they will be making predictions, or educated guesses, about what might happen in the story, and they will base their predictions on the title, illustrations, and what they read in preceding sections. They will read up to, but not beyond, the stopping points and will not read ahead. They will justify their predictions based on what they learn as the story unfolds. All predictions will be accepted respectfully by everyone. The process of predicting, not whether their predictions are proved or disproved, is what is important.

4. Have students read the title, examine cover art and initial illustrations, and perhaps the first section of the story. Elicit predictions by asking, "What might happen in this story?" or "What might this story be about?" and "Why do you think so?" Jot down key phrases from different predictions. Have students read the next section to find out and stop at the next stopping point.

5. After each section, have students briefly review what they know so far and new information revealed in the prior section. Review and check predictions that still seem likely or possible. Elicit further predictions about the next section.

6. Repeat this cycle of "review-predict-read to prove" to the end. At the conclusion of the story, briefly discuss with students how they used clues and events to predict the outcome.

Variation: Read the story aloud to the group as a Directed Listening-Thinking Activity, following the same procedures.

27. Dual-Entry Diary

Objectives: To develop comprehension of and response to reading material

Materials: Journals, literature or reading logs, or sheets of paper divided vertically down the middle

Duration: 5–10 minutes

1. Have students draw a line down the middle of a page in their journals or reading logs. On the left side of the line they write a summary statement, interesting line of dialogue, or a very short excerpt from the text that made them respond in some important way: It surprised them, it answered a previous question they had, it confused or baffled them, it reminded them of something important, or it caused an emotional response in some way. Students can write and/or sketch on the left side.

2. On the right side, directly across from the previous entry, students write a response or comment about it, explaining what they were thinking about and why. What did the left-side entry make them think about, remind them of, or make them wonder? Why did they select it? What makes it interesting, intriguing, or important?

3. Students can share their entries orally with a partner, small sharing group, or the larger group. They can also trade journals with a partner and write a brief, uncritical comment or question about their partner's entry, or the teacher can read and comment on the entries in the same way.

Variations: Students who are reading the same book or story with others can create a journal entry for each chapter or section of the material as the group proceeds, and read and comment on each other's entries as part of the group discussion of the text. Entries should be dated or labeled by chapter or section. With fiction, left-side entries can include a brief summary of the most important events of the preceding section, and right-side entries can include predictions of what might happen in the next section.

28. Save the Last Word for Me

Objectives: To develop comprehension; encourage thoughtful discussion of a shared text

Materials: 3 × 5 file cards or sheets of paper cut in quarters; 1–4 cards per student

Duration: 10–20 minutes depending on size of group

1. Distribute blank file cards or papers to students.

2. After they have finished reading a selection, have them find a sentence or short section (no longer than a few sentences, or as short as one sentence) in the text that they find particularly interesting, surprising, evocative, or otherwise noteworthy and write the quotation on one side of a card. On the reverse side they write a comment or response: why they found it interesting, what it made them think about, something it reminded them of, and so forth. Older students and those reading longer or more complex texts can complete several cards in the same way; younger readers or those reading shorter texts can complete one.

3. When completed, ask a volunteer to read his or her selected quotation aloud and call on several other students to comment on or respond to the quotation. Discussion of each other's comments is allowed. After several others have commented, the first student shares his or her written comment on the quotation. No discussion follows; the original writer has "the last word."

4. Another student is selected by the first student or the teacher to repeat the procedure; read the quotation, invite others to comment, then share his or her written comment. In small discussion groups or literature circles, all students may be able to participate; in larger groups or with the whole class, only some will be able to share each time.

29. Literature Circles

Objectives: To develop comprehension; promote thoughtful discussion and interpretation of shared literature

Materials: A shared work of literature (all students in the group read the same text)

Duration: 20 minutes or longer, depending on the group size, degree of experience with the procedure, and students' interest in discussion

1. Assign students participating to read the same text; they may read a short text in one sitting or read a section such as a chapter of a longer work.

2. Convene a group of all the students reading the shared work; for best interaction, group size should not exceed 5 or 6. If more students are reading the same text, create two groups.

3. Assign each student a role for that meeting; see textbook, Figure 6.4, for a list of possible roles. The roles most often used include the Questioner, sometimes called the Discussion Director, who creates three or four thoughtful questions about the main events of the selection for the group to discuss; the Quotation Finder, sometimes called the Passage Master, who selects one or more excerpts to practice and read aloud; the Artist, or Illustrator, who illustrates the selection with written captions; and the Word Finder, or Word Wizard, who locates and explains interesting or important words, figurative language, expressions or idioms, and the like, to the group.

4. Monitor the execution of the various roles in the group discussion; model reflective questioning and responding to the text without lecturing or dominating; move the discussion forward when necessary by drawing all students into the discussion, and use literary terms such as *episode*, *climax*, *resolution*, and so forth, as appropriate.

5. If students are reading a longer work in sections, assist them in deciding how far they will read before the next meeting and when they will next meet.

6. Have all students regardless of their role write a summary, response, or other piece in their literature or reading journals about the section just discussed.

7. Rotate the roles so all students participate and have different responsibilities.

30. Discussion Web

Objectives: To develop comprehension; promote thoughtful discussion and interpretation of shared literature; help students perceive and understand both sides of a position or argument

Materials: A shared work of literature (all students in the group read the same text)

Duration: 15–30 minutes

1. Assign students participating to read the same text; they may read a short text in one sitting or read a section such as a chapter of a longer work. Text may be fiction or nonfiction.

2. Generate a discussion question that can reasonably be argued from both sides, sometimes called a binary question; for example, "Was it wrong for _____ (story character) to _____ (act in a way that some might consider wrong, but for which he or she had a reason or rationale)?" "Was _____ (story character) _____ or _____ (two opposite or opposing characteristics, like brave/reckless, caring/selfish, or wise/foolish)?" or "Is (or was) it right or wrong to _____ (nonfiction text or subject area issue: secede from the Union, hunt whales, log the rain forest, send Japanese Americans to internment camps, etc.)?" Write the question so students can refer to it as they reflect.

3. Assign students to pairs. Have each pair answer the question from both sides of the argument, listing three reasons, examples, and so forth, to support each side.

4. Combine two pairs to create groups of four. Have students combine their lists so all positions are included. Then have each foursome reach agreement on one side of the argument and prepare to defend it.

5. Have each foursome summarize and defend its work to the larger group.

Extension: When two or more groups take opposing positions, a formal debate can follow. Groups taking the same position can join forces to share arguments and prepare to present them as forcefully and logically as possible, prepare notes, select spokespersons, and if desired conduct research on their position. Establish strict ground rules (no personal attacks, no raised voices, etc.) and time limits for arguments and rebuttal. Have each side briefly summarize its arguments in closing.

31. Story Maps

Objectives: To develop comprehension; help students identify and sequence key story elements and events

Materials: Shared fiction text; story map graphic organizer, with key story elements for students to label

Duration: 10–20 minutes

1. Have students read, or read to them, a well-structured story that has a clear plot line including a well-defined main character; a problem, goal, challenge, or defining event faced by the main character; a series of attempts by the character to solve the problem or achieve the goal, the first several of which are unsuccessful, often referred to as the *rising action*; a final attempt that is successful, although not always as the character expected, forming the climax; and a resolution of the story, in which the character is often changed in some way.

2. Create a simple graphic organizer that labels the major parts of the story and allows students to fill in spaces on a chart, timeline, or flowchart. (There are many different kinds of premade story map graphic organizers available in teacher resource books, textbooks, basal manuals, comprehension kits, and so forth, or you can make your own.) For emergent and beginning readers, divide a sheet of paper into thirds vertically and label the sections *Beginning*, *Middle*, and *End*; students retell the story, then draw a picture to represent each part and write or dictate one or two sentences telling what happened in that part.

3. Have students include important details supporting the plot, including the setting and supporting characters.

4. Allow students to share their story maps by using them to retell the story.

Extensions: Provide students free access to a variety of types of story maps they can complete as they finish a work of fiction. Carefully completed story maps can be substituted for book reports or reviews when students must demonstrate their comprehension of a completed story. They can be shared during oral book reports. When students are writing fiction, completing a story map during the planning stage of the writing cycle helps students plan a complete story before they start and helps them structure their stories. (See "Story Maps for Writing" activity.)

32. Character Clusters and Character Maps

Objectives: To develop comprehension; help students understand characteristics or traits of story characters and relationships among characters

Materials: Shared work of fiction; chalkboard, transparency, or chart paper

Duration: 10–15 minutes

A. Character Cluster

1. Have students identify the main character in a shared work of fiction. (If a work has more than one central character, create a separate cluster for each main character.)

2. Create a web graphic organizer by placing the main character's name in a circle in the center of the web. Have students brainstorm characteristics or traits of that character (e.g., brave, funny, a loyal friend, loves wildlife, shy, etc.). Have students select three to five that are most descriptive of that character and write those traits in circles around the center circle, connected to it by lines.

3. For each characteristic, have students generate examples of the character's words, actions, and attitudes from the story that illustrate that trait. Write these examples in circles that are connected by lines to the trait circles; for example, *brave*: chased away the mean dog, told the truth about breaking the lamp.

B. Character Map

1. List with students the main and supporting characters in a work of fiction they have read or are reading. Have students identify the main character/s.

2. Write the names of the main character in a central circle and the supporting characters in circles arranged around the central one. (Leave plenty of writing space between the circles.) Have students briefly describe how the main character feels about the supporting character. Draw an arrow from the main character to a supporting character; along the line, write a sentence that describes those feelings. Repeat for the other supporting characters.

3. With student help as above, draw arrows from the supporting characters to the main character and to other supporting characters. Along the arrows, write these characters' feelings about each other.

Comprehension Activities
with Nonfictional Texts

33. Think-Pair-Share

Objectives: To reflect on and thoughtfully respond to a question and share responses with a peer; encourage reflective thinking and respectful listening; develop comprehension by recalling and organizing prior information before reading

Materials: Students may write their initial responses in journals or learning logs or on scrap paper; otherwise, no materials are needed

Duration: 5 minutes or less

1. Ask an open-ended question—that is, a question that can be answered many ways depending on the opinions, experiences, predictions, or preferences of the individuals answering it. For example; "What could we do as a class to show our concern for the environment?" "How could this story character have behaved differently so the story had a different outcome?" or "What traits or characteristics make a person a good leader?" Write the question so students can reread it as they think.

2. Have students think, then write in brief form their thoughts in their journals, learning logs, or on scrap paper.

3. After a short interval for writing, have each student turn to a partner and share his or her answers to the questions, taking turns. Remind students to talk to their partners, not read their papers to them, and to listen respectfully and attentively to each other.

4. Have a few volunteers share their thoughts with the larger group or restate their partner's response instead of their own.

Variation: *Paired Brainstorming* In a situation where students will share factual information, for example before reading expository text when students are recalling and organizing their prior information about the topic, have individuals briefly list the information they already know during the "Think" phase. After a minute or two, each student joins a partner and the two lists are quickly combined during the "Pair" stage. Finally, a few key facts from each pair are listed on the board, chart paper, or a transparency during the "Share" stage. Students can compare what they knew before reading to information they acquire during and after reading.

34. Anticipation Guide

Objectives: To develop comprehension by recalling and organizing prior information before reading

Materials: Teacher-made anticipation guides, duplicated for each student

Duration: 5–10 minutes to complete the guide prior to reading and again after reading the material

1. Read through the material your students are going to read. Select a number of important facts, terms, and so forth, you want students to remember and understand from the reading.

2. Create a set of statements to which students will respond by agreeing or disagreeing, marking them True or False, or checking the statements they think are true; for example, "There were thirteen southern colonies," "Maple syrup is made by crushing the leaves of the maple tree," or "Only native-born U.S. citizens can become president."

3. Type each statement, preceding each one with a blank on the left side of the paper and following each one with a blank on the right side of the paper. Head the left-side column of blanks "BEFORE" and the right-hand column "AFTER."

4. Distribute the anticipation guides *before* reading or discussing the text material, and have students read and mark each statement true/false, agree/disagree, and so forth, in the BEFORE (before reading) column. (Be sure they understand they are not expected to know all the right answers, just to make an attempt at each item based on what, if anything, they might already know about the topic, and their answers will not be corrected, graded, etc.) Collect the guides and keep them for later. Briefly discuss students' responses to each statement, but do not tell them the correct answer.

5. Read and discuss the text material as you would normally do. After students have thoroughly read and discussed the material, participated in comprehension activities, and so forth, redistribute the original anticipation guides and have students respond to each item, this time marking in the AFTER (after reading) column. These responses should now represent the correct information; therefore, answers in the AFTER column may be checked for correctness or graded. Be sure students understand that their initial attempts were "best guesses," and only their responses after the reading will be checked.

6. Students can fold the BEFORE column under and keep their anticipation guides as a form of class notes or study guides on the topic.

35. Graphic Organizers

Objectives: To help students organize information in text

Materials: Blank graphic organizers for students to fill in before, during, and after reading

Duration: 5–30 minutes depending on length and complexity of text and the graphic organizer used

1. Select or create a graphic organizer that fits the organization of the text: for example, a timeline or sequential flowchart for sequences of events, Venn diagram for comparison/contrast, or web for main and subordinate categories.

2. Have students preview or skim the material to find some of the main topics or categories of information and enter them on the graphic organizer. With textbook material, chapter headings and subheads often contain this information.

3. Have students attempt to recall and organize their prior information about these topics before reading, and note what they already know in pencil on the organizer. (If they are later disproved, these entries can easily be changed.)

4. As students read, they continue to enter new information they encounter on the organizer: for example, dates and places of historical events, short- and long-term effects of events, biographical information, and other important supporting details.

5. After the reading, have students compare their organizers in pairs or small groups, adding or moving information as needed to make their organizers clear and accurate. They can then be used as outlines for writing or for study guides.

36. Know-Want to Know-Learn (K-W-L)

Objectives: To develop comprehension by recalling and organizing prior information before reading; organize new information gained by reading and relate it to prior information

Materials: Nonfiction material; chalkboard, chart paper, or transparency; duplicated KWL charts

Duration: 10–30 minutes or longer, depending on length of selection and students' prior information

1. Create a KWL chart on the board, chart paper, or transparency consisting of three vertical columns; label the left-side column K: What We Know, the center column W: What We Want to Find Out; and the right-side column L: What We Learned. Write the topic at the top. Duplicate and distribute blank charts.

2. Prior to reading, have students write some things they already know about the topic in the K column on their charts. Have volunteers share some of their ideas; record them in the K column on the group chart. Ask direct questions about important information in the passage that no one mentioned.

3. When disagreements occur or when questions arise that can't be answered prior to reading, note these in the W column. Have students generate and write on their charts one question they can't answer; write some of these on the group chart and have students include them on their charts as well.

4. Briefly review with students what they already know and are uncertain about. Read the passage.

5. After reading, review the K column with students; check those ideas that were borne out by the passage; and cross off those that were disproved, writing the correct information in the L column. Review the W column; check those questions that were answered by the passage, writing the corresponding information in the L column. Mark those questions still unanswered with a question mark for further research. Add to the L column any other new information gathered from the passage.

6. Have students reorganize and add to their own charts as you do so with the group chart.

37. What? So What? Now What?

Objectives: To help students organize facts and arguments to prepare to do persuasive writing or speaking

Materials: Blank organizer on board, chart paper, or transparency; duplicated copies of blank organizer for students to complete

Duration: 10–15 minutes

1. Prepare a model organizer for the group to complete on the board, chart paper, or a transparency. Create three columns across the top: label the left-side column WHAT?, the center column SO WHAT?, and the right-side column NOW WHAT? Explain that this chart will help them organize their facts and opinions to write or speak persuasively on an issue they have read about (e.g., environmental pollution, species endangerment, cafeteria recycling, logging of national forest lands, etc.).

2. On the left side of the chart, list factual information students have learned about the topic: for example, "Since 1950, ___ species have become endangered and ___ have become extinct," or "Species are now becoming endangered at an average rate of ____." In the central column, list students' reasons why these facts are important or why others should care about them. In the right-side column, write students' suggestions of actions that could affect or improve the situation.

3. Using the completed group chart, have students compose persuasive essays or speeches presenting the relevant facts, explaining their importance, and urging their audience to pursue a course of action.

Variations: When an issue arises that students care about, complete this chart with them to help them sort out facts from opinions, create persuasive arguments, and determine how they can act on their beliefs. Then follow through as a group on one or more actions to address the situation.

Extensions: Have students organize the information in the L column in categories and construct a web or other graphic organizer of the information. Have students use their KWL charts as study guides or as resources for writing summaries and reports. Gather related reading materials and have students research answers to questions still listed in the W column. Follow up with a "What? So What? Now What?" activity to help students determine actions that can be taken based on what they learned.

38. Reciprocal Teaching

Objectives: To model and practice comprehension strategies of summarizing, questioning, clarifying, and predicting

Materials: Nonfiction text; chalkboard, chart paper or transparency

Duration: 15–30 minutes or longer, depending on length and difficulty of text

1. Survey and break the text into segments for students to read; depending on the length and difficulty of the entire selection, segments may be as short as one or two paragraphs or as long as a chapter section. Students can use sticky notes to mark the end of a segment. Create groups of four students each.

2. Read the first segment with students. Then model how to use the four strategies: First, summarize the section in one or two sentences, writing them on the board, chart paper, or transparency; second, ask one or two good questions to be answered by students; third, clarify by identifying the most difficult part of the section (may be a word or phrase, sentence, example, or concept) and explain it or tell how you could figure it out (look it up, check an encyclopedia, use surrounding context, etc.); fourth, predict what the next section might contain based on what you've already read.

3. Assign each student in a group a task for the next section: summarizer, questioner, clarifier, or predictor. (Job cards help students remember what they are to do.) Read the next section with students.

4. After reading, each student is to complete his or her task following your model. Allow time for task completion. Each student then shares his or her work with the group, starting with the summary statement and ending with the prediction. The group should discuss and amend the summary as needed, use the text to answer the questions, examine the difficult part and add to the explanation, and discuss the prediction.

5. Repeat the teacher modeling of the strategies after reading the next section. Depending on time available and students' success with the procedure, you can continue to alternate teacher modeling and student practice through the remaining sections or have students work through subsequent sections as above, rotating tasks within the group so each student completes a different task each time.

Writing Activities

39. Shared Writing

Objectives: To engage students in composing a written text
Materials: Chart paper
Duration: 10–15 minutes

1. Choose a topic that the children are excited about (e.g., a field trip).

2. Ask the students to offer comments about the topic.

3. Write down their comments on the chart paper.

4. As you write, ask students to sound out some of the words and to offer spellings for them.

40. Interactive Writing

Objectives: To help emergent and beginning readers and writers explore the writing system in its details

Materials: Chart paper

Duration: 15–20 minutes

1. Working with a medium-size group of students, begin by agreeing on a topic to write about. The topic might be a retelling of a story or a poem or a song, the daily news, or an idea that the class is studying.

2. Ask the children to offer a sentence about the topic.

3. Have them repeat the sentence many times and even count the words to fix them firmly in their minds.

4. Ask the children for the first word; then pronounce that word slowly, writing its letters.

5. Ask for the next word and invite a child up to write the whole word, a few letters, or a single letter. Fill in letters the children miss.

6. Point to the words and have the children read back the text. Repeat this step each time a word is added.

7. To help the children orient themselves to the text and add letters, you may write blanks where the letters should go.

8. Use correction tape to paste over letters that are poorly formed, and write them correctly.

9. As the lesson progresses, teach about words and print (remind children of words they know or almost know, remind them of spelling patterns they have seen before, remind them to leave spaces between words, and to add punctuation).

41. Pillowcase, or Me in a Box

Objectives: To introduce yourself to students by displaying objects representing aspects of your life; encourage discussion; provide springboard for personal writing

Materials: Pillowcase, bag, box, or similar container; objects representing your interests, family, pets, hobbies, and so forth, in a container

Duration: 5–10 minutes to share and discuss objects; extended time for discussion and/or writing

1. Collect a number of objects that represent things about you to share with students: for example, photos, sports trophy, dog toy, college banner, map, vacation postcards, and so forth. Put them in the container.

2. Explain that the objects you collected tell about you as a person. As you show each object, explain what it represents.

3. Have students write or dictate a few sentences about you based on what they learned.

4. Invite students to collect objects in the same way and tell the group about themselves. Schedule a few talks per day so students know when to bring in their things. (Remind them to get parents' permission before bringing anything valuable or personal to school.)

5. Have students use their collections to help them write about themselves.

Variations: Invite other teachers, the principal, or other school personnel to share in the same way. Have students draw self-portraits, or use a digital camera or school pictures from cumulative files to illustrate their writing. Collect the compositions in a class book. Display them in or outside the classroom. Make a "Students of the Week" bulletin board to display several students' writings at a time until all have been displayed. Create a web graphic organizer as you model this activity; write your name in the center, the objects in circles around it, and words or phrases explaining the objects projecting from the circles. Show how the web can help you organize your writing.

42. The Writing Workshop

Objectives: To familiarize students with the writing process

Materials: Notebooks

Duration: Sessions of 30–60 minutes scheduled at regular intervals over a longer period of time, with time set aside for five distinct activities in each session

1. Rehearsing. Have students think of what they might like to write about. You can do this in one of the ways listed below. For a–c, demonstrate how you yourself would settle on a topic.

   a. Have the students brainstorm possible topics. Optionally, have them create a graphic organizer, such as a cluster or semantic web, with the topic listed in the center connected to "satellites" around it.

   b. Have the students interview each other to find a story.

   c. Have the students research a topic before they write about it (by reading about it, by interviewing experts, or by doing an Internet search).

   d. Ask the students to compose one work together as a class before writing their own. This will allow you to help them if they have difficulty beginning.

2. Drafting. Have the students set out their ideas on paper, so they can see more of what they want to say about a topic. Tell them not to worry about spelling, punctuation, and handwriting at this stage. Remember to tell the students to write on every other line, so they can make subsequent changes to the draft.

3. Revising. Have students consider how their ideas can be stated more clearly. Teach revising skills through the following:

   a. Focused lessons on different aspects of writing, from word-choice issues such as showing, not telling, to composition-related issues such as ways to write strong introductions and closings. In one of the early focused lessons, show students how to use arrows, carets (^), and stapled-on sections to indicate on a draft how it should be rewritten. Remember to demonstrate how you would revise your own draft each time.

   b. Teacher-led conferences with groups or individual students. Ask students questions to help them focus on areas to improve their writing, and provide checklists of things to watch out for.

c. Peer-led conferences. Put together a checklist of good questions to ask as students conference with each other, such as the following:

- Did my opening lines interest you? How might I improve it?
- Do I need more information anywhere? That is, where could I be more specific?
- Do you ever get lost while reading my draft?
- Do I stay on topic?
- Do I come to a good conclusion?

4.   Editing. Have the students check their revised drafts for spelling, punctuation, run-on sentences, and so forth.

5.   Publishing/Sharing of work in progress. Choose two or three students to share who are far along in a draft or whose work displays an interesting issue. Different students should share each time. Model giving feedback to the writers and elicit comments from the class.

43. Descriptive Writing

Objectives: To familiarize students with genre of descriptive writing; provide practice in descriptive writing

Materials: Excerpt from text that is vividly descriptive; paper bag containing a concrete object; journals or writing folders

Duration: 15–30 minutes depending on length of text excerpt and size of group

1. Select a descriptive passage, fiction or nonfiction, to read aloud. The passage should exemplify good descriptive writing.

2. Place an object in a paper bag for students to feel without looking at it. It should be small and light enough to be held in one hand, unusual enough so students may not recognize it instantly, and safe to feel without looking (no sharp edges, points, etc.).

3. Read the excerpt to the group. Invite students' comments about how the author used vivid descriptive language. Discuss the author's use of sensory words and images to create description.

4. Have students take turns silently feeling the object in the bag without looking at it. Caution them not to say what they think it is or what it feels like. After feeling the object, each one is to brainstorm and write in journals descriptive words or phrases to describe the object without naming it. Then they are to use their list of words to write descriptive sentences or a paragraph about the object, again without saying what it is.

5. Have students share their descriptive writing before naming the object.

Variations: Use senses other than touch to explore an object; with eyes closed, have students sniff objects like a sliced orange, blooming flower, cinnamon stick or other edible spice, school paste, ground coffee, pine or eucalyptus branch; listen to environmental or recorded sounds like wind, flowing water, heavy machinery, rain, surf, traffic; or taste safe and edible substances like toothpaste, coarse sugar, dry gelatin powder, baking chocolate, or pickles. Collect, or have students collect, small objects like keys, erasers, shells, bottle caps, or toys, and place one on each desk; give students a few minutes to write a complete description of the object, and then switch objects with someone else and repeat. Have students write what an object reminds them of rather than describing its physical features alone.

44. Story Maps for Writing

Objectives: To assist writers in planning a cohesive story

Materials: Blank story map on board, chart paper, or transparency; duplicated copies of the blank map for students to complete as they plan their stories

Duration: 5–15 minutes

1. On the board, chart paper, or a transparency, construct a story map containing elements similar to the following: Once there was a _____ named _____ who lived _____. He/she wanted _____. So he/she _____, but _____ (so he/she _____, but _____). Then, he/she _____. Finally, _____. So, _____. Leave plenty of space after each sentence starter.

2. Invite students to help you plan to write a story by suggesting elements to go in each blank space; for example, a boy named Sam who lived in a small apartment in the city, who wanted a dog, so he asked his parents . . . and so forth. Remind students that the story elements they suggest need to fit together to make sense. Select suggestions to write in the blanks that will make a meaningful story. To set off the sentence starters from the rest of the text, use a different color to complete the sentences.

3. Read through the completed story map, showing students where details could be added that would help readers visualize the story. Focus attention on the character's problem or goal, attempts to solve the problem or achieve the goal, and the final resolution of the conflict. Display the group story for students to refer to as they write.

4. Distribute blank story maps and have students generate their own stories, filling in the blanks to create a skeletal story. Allow time to share ideas and completed plans with partners or small groups.

5. Have students write their stories following their story maps. Encourage them to write several sentences or a paragraph after each sentence starter, to discourage them from recopying their maps as completed stories. Allow time for sharing of completed stories.

Variations: Before attempting to write a story solo, allow pairs to create a shared story after participating in the group story. Encourage students to revise, edit, and illustrate their stories, then display or publish them. Collect illustrated stories in a binder and place in the classroom library.

45. Form Poems

Objectives: To familiarize students with structured poems; increase students' awareness of how form and meaning can shape each other in poetry

Materials: Examples of form poems

Duration: 10–20 minutes

1. Show the students an example of a well-written poem that follows the form. (You might need to write this yourself or save it from a previous class.)

2. Discuss the formal characteristics of the poem with the class.

3. Have the students help you create a poem as a group. Discuss each choice they make so they understand the process well.

4. Have individuals or pairs write their own poems.

5. Share several of the poems, and discuss their qualities. Also call attention to the ways in which the poems followed the structure.

6. Talk about why a writer might choose to write a poem structured that way.

7. Make a wall chart in which you feature several of the students' poems; also outline the procedures for writing a poem with the structure in question.

Activities for English-Language Learners

46. Language Experience with English-Language Learners

Objectives: To help English-language learners develop English fluency, print concepts, sight word recognition, and phonemic awareness

Materials: An object, photograph, shared experience, shared literature, or other stimulus; chalkboard, chart tablet, or transparency; marker

Duration: 10–30 minutes; additional time for follow-up activities

1. Select an individual student or a group of English-language learners.

2. Select a topic for dictation: an interesting concrete object, classroom pet, familiar story for retelling, recent classroom event, and so forth. Younger students benefit from a concrete or immediate stimulus, whereas older students can talk about past events, friends, families, and other more abstract topics. Encourage students to select topics.

3. Explain that you can write what students say, that they can learn to read what was written, and that learning words in these sentences will help them learn to read and write many other words.

4. Invite discussion of the stimulus, encouraging students to use as elaborated language as they can. Ask open-ended questions that encourage extended answers. If students give brief or incomplete sentences, model elaborated language using their words: S: "Green. Fuzzy." T: "It's green and fuzzy."

5. Ask for volunteers to contribute sentences for the dictation.

6. Write students' sentences, allowing changes or additions. If you want students to learn to read each other's names, include their names in the text. Print neatly with clear spaces between each word.

7. Read the completed story expressively and at a natural pace, pointing to each word as you read.

8. Reread the story chorally several times until students have memorized it. Continue pointing to each word. (Keep up the pace so the reading sounds natural, not word by word.) If students have trouble memorizing the whole text, divide it into sections of two or three sentences each.

9. Invite volunteers to come to the chart and recite a part or the whole story while pointing to each word. Continue until each student who volunteers has read the story individually.

10. Point to individual words and invite students to identify the words, reading from the beginning to the target word if necessary.

Follow-Up Activities for English-Language Learners

1. Repeat choral and individual reading and pointing on subsequent days until students can read the story fluently and point accurately. (Older students can reread and point using duplicated copies of the story rather than at a chart.)

2. Copy each sentence onto a sentence strip. Have volunteers hold up each strip in correct order. (These can also be used for independent practice with a hanging pocket chart.)

3. Create exact copies of the story on copy paper. Duplicate several copies for each student. Students can paste copies on construction paper or in journals and illustrate them, cut lines and sentences apart and put them in correct order, cut sentences into phrases and put them in correct order, and use sentences for handwriting practice.

4. Have students find individual words they recognize in isolation and begin building individual word banks with known words on cards. Students should sort and review word banks daily.

5. Have students sort words in their word banks in a variety of ways: matching beginning sounds, number of syllables, alphabetical order, words that are related by meaning, and so forth.

6. Select one or several familiar words beginning with consonants. Using individual letter cards or magnetic letters, show students how to "make and break" the words by removing the initial letter or sound and substituting another, creating new words.

7. Students can write known sight words using magnetic letters on cookie sheets, individual letters cut out of sandpaper, wallpaper scraps, felt, glue and sand or glitter, pipe cleaners, gel pens, macaroni letters, letters cut from magazines, and so forth. They can also search for known words in newspaper and magazine ads and headlines, and cut them out.

8. Begin personal dictionaries by folding eight to ten sheets of paper vertically and stapling in the fold to create individual books. Have students write a letter at the top of each page (group infrequent letters like q, u, x, y, and z with others) and begin collecting mastered sight words in their dictionaries.

9. As students' word banks grow, have them construct sentences with word cards.

47. Cumulative Semantic Map

Objectives: To foster vocabulary growth; help students learn meanings of
related words

Materials: Large paper chart that can be displayed and added to periodically

Duration: 5–15 minutes each time new words are added

1. Have students begin collecting words that are related by meaning: for
   example, synonyms, color words, action words, and so forth.

2. Construct a web graphic organizer on the chart, with one or more general
   categories in the center and related words radiating from them. For
   example, a cumulative semantic web on temperature words might show
   HOT and COLD in central circles, with various temperature words attached
   to them: *burning, boiling, sizzling, blistering, icy, freezing, frigid, polar,*
   and so forth.

3. As students encounter related words in their reading, or as you encounter
   such words in literature you read to them, return to the web and have
   students suggest where such words might be added or where new categories
   might be entered. For example, a new category of WARM words could be
   added, to include *comfortable, mild, tepid,* and *lukewarm.*

4. Encourage students to use words from the charts in their writing and to
   continue to watch for words that could be added to the collection.

48. Word Origins and Derivations

Objectives: To develop vocabulary; teach meanings of bases and affixes to help students figure out meanings of unfamiliar words; engage students in language learning

Materials: Space for Word Walls, charts, and bulletin board words; paper and markers; resource materials (dictionaries that include word histories, thesauruses, books on idioms, etc.)

Duration: 10–15 minutes several times weekly

1. Encourage students to begin collecting words they need to learn for subject areas and interesting or unfamiliar words they encounter during reading. Have them copy the sentence in which the word occurs, or share the text, so they can practice using context as a meaning clue. Make a Word Wall or chart of student-selected words, their context sentences, and meanings.

2. Teach vocabulary words in groups that have a shared base or affix; for example, *ex-*(out): *exhale, exclaim, expand, exorcise, expectorate, exfoliate, explode, expire*; *in-/im-/il-*(not): *illiterate, illogical, illegal, illegible, immature, imbalance, impassable, immortal, incapable, inappropriate, inaudible, inconvenient.* Create word families and add new words as students encounter them.

3. Teach the meanings of the Latin and Greek bases or stems that have consistent meanings: for example, *photo* (light) , *graph* (write), *mega* (large), *cap* (head), *corp* (body), *ped* (foot), *manu* (hand), *scrib* (write), *retro* (backward), *poly* (many), *phone* (sound), *mono* (single), *bi* (two), *tri* (three), *cent* (hundred). Draw attention to these word parts and their meanings whenever they occur.

4. Avoid having students copy dictionary definitions, which they rarely understand. Instead, have them predict a word's meaning from word parts they know and context sentences before looking it up. Have them write meanings in their own words rather than a dictionary definition.

5. Have students divide word cards into three sections to include (a) the word, (b) its meaning in their own words, and (c) synonyms and opposites. On the back have them draw a sketch that illustrates the meaning, and write a caption for the drawing.

6. Limit the number of new words students have to learn each week; teach a group of related words and have students really learn fewer words rather than superficially memorize a long list.

49. Visualization

Objectives: To develop comprehension; model and practice visualizing or mentally seeing images a writer creates with words

Materials: Shared text; reading journals or literature logs; duplicated copies of the text that students can draw on; sticky notes; pencils

Duration: 5 minutes or less at various points in a text

1. Copy a short (1–2 paragraphs) excerpt of vivid or descriptive text onto the board, chart paper, or a transparency. Explain that you will model what good readers do as they visualize text.

2. Read the passage expressively; as you read it, pause and think aloud by telling students what you are mentally seeing or imagining. Mark the words, phrases, or sentences that are particularly vivid to you. Make a quick sketch in the margin that represents what you are visualizing, and explain what it means to you.

3. Distribute duplicated copies of similar text or portions of a text students are reading together. Read aloud a short section while students follow along. Have volunteers say what they visualized as you read, following your model. Have all students sketch in the margin as above, or distribute sticky notes and have students sketch on them and place them over or near the appropriate sections. Ask each student to tell briefly what they drew; they do not need to display the drawings because they are a sort of personal code.

4. In later lessons, students can write ("jot") what they are visualizing, using brief phrases, in addition to or instead of sketching. Students may prefer one method over the other; neither one is "better."

Variations: As students read longer or more difficult passages, encourage them to use the "jot" or "sketch" methods independently to help them visualize by making sticky notes available during reading, by having them jot or sketch in their reading journals at the end of each day's reading, and by periodically repeating the activity with different kinds of text. Use visualization in combination with the Think-Pair-Share activity; after visualizing and drawing, each student shares with a single partner and then each pair with another pair. Encourage students to use sketches, drawings, or cutout magazine pictures to illustrate their writing about what they are reading.

50. Using Questions to Teach English-Language Learners

Objectives: Vocabulary development; to help students learning English to acquire words, follow directions, and converse with others

Materials: Props to talk about: magazine pictures, picture cards, small objects like keys, toy cars, plastic fruit and other foods from children's kitchen toys, puppets, stuffed animals, and so forth

Duration: 5–15 minutes or longer, depending on students' age, English fluency, and size of group

1. Select a group of students who are similar in English fluency. Gather pictures or props to use.

2. Determine the general fluency level of students and plan the activity to meet their English abilities: preproduction, where students understand a few words but speak little; early production, where students understand simple sentences and produce very short utterances; or speech emergence, where students understand many words and sentences and produce longer, more varied sentences.

3. For preproduction students, use very simple, repetitive sentences accompanied by gesture and sound effects: "This is an apple. Is it red? Yes, it's red. Is it green? No, not green." "Can Maria hold the apple? Yes, she can. Can Nguyen hold the apple? Yes, he can. Can I hold the apple? Yes, I can." "Who has a frog? Juan has a frog. Who has a bird? Irma has a bird."

4. For early production students, use questions that require short answers, including yes/no, here/there, either/or, how many . . . , what color . . . , and common prepositions like in/out/under: "Is this a dog or a bird? What color is the bird? Do you like birds?" "Is this the mother or the father? Where is the baby? How many children are there?"

5. For speech emergence students, ask questions requiring longer answers, description, and simple sentences. Use wordless picture books, tell what is happening on each page, and ask students to retell. Read simple versions of stories several times, and have students retell or act out the stories using puppets or a flannel board. Play direction-following games like Simon Says, and have students give each other directions to follow: Stand behind your chair; open and close the door; raise your left hand. Practice naming objects: foods, clothing, tools, vehicles, classroom objects, colors, temperature words, animals, family members, areas of the school and home, and people (teacher, principal, nurse, bus driver).

NOTES